To Nanny and Grandad for
Joe, Le
e Ian ✗

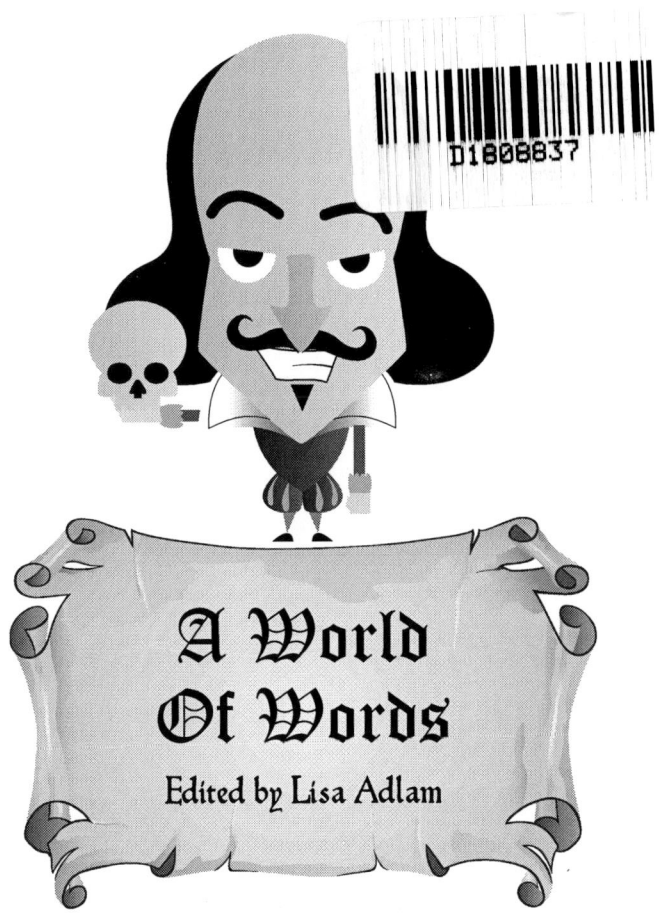

YoungWriters

Shake-up Shakespeare

A World Of Words

Edited by Lisa Adlam

D1808837

First published in Great Britain in 2015 by:

 Young**Writers**

Remus House
Coltsfoot Drive
Peterborough
PE2 9BF
Telephone: 01733 890066
Website: www.youngwriters.co.uk

All Rights Reserved
Book Design by Spencer Hart
© Copyright Contributors 2015
ISBN 978-1-78443-941-5

Printed and bound in the UK by BookPrintingUK
Website: www.bookprintinguk.com

Foreword

Young Writers was established in 1991 to promote poetry and nurture the creative writing talent in school children across the UK and overseas. Today we continue to provide a platform for children and young adults to showcase their work.

For our latest anthology we asked young writers to compose a poem to celebrate Shakespeare Day on 23rd April. With 38 plays, 154 sonnets and numerous other poems, William Shakespeare is widely regarded as the greatest writer in the English language. His plays are performed more often than those of any other playwright and he invented over 1,500 words that are still used today. Who better then to inspire our poets of the future?

The poems in this collection are inspired by Shakespeare's life, his plays and his poetry, showing that nearly 400 years after his death his work is still relevant and a source of inspiration for poets of the future.

Contents

Bacon's College, London

Beeslack High School, Penicuik

Benedict Biscop CE Academy, Sunderland

Birralee International School, Trondeim

Coopersale Hall School, Epping

Great Chart Primary School, Ashford

Harvington Prep School, London

Ide Hill CE Primary School, Sevenoaks

John Spendluffe Technology College, Alford

Laycock Primary School, London

St Edward's Royal Free Ecumenical Middle School, Windsor

St Hilda's CE High School, Liverpool

Shrivenham CE Primary School, Swindon

The King's School, Witney

The Pines School, Bracknell

The Redhill Academy, Nottingham

The Poems

Lady Macbeth's Last Integrity

O! Harvest O . . . bitter harvest
Macbeth requests my presence
My vengeance's sweet sorrow.
The kingship is close to my bosom
My delicate hands sense the treasure
That pierced dagger strikes the fortune, as it changes fate
Blood onto blood from one's supposed mate.
I flee into the fruitful grasslands, I soak up the newborn air,
Standing in awe of the domineering painting that lies before me, the dashing rawness of the elongated robe
Impossibly painted by a lion cub, everyone's 'Thane of Cawdor'
Beneath it all sown by irresistible whispered oaths, sternness in one's eye
It is the dagger that truly sheds blood for me.
O the deity doth tease me so, like the rich air
I breathe in through my nose, unconsciously
Finds a way of escaping through my mouth, my
Definite words in vain, I hesitate to stretch out my gnawing hands,
I must embed it,
But what use are these commoner's hands?
O silver lining, O demeaning yet powerful silver lining,
Sigh and sigh again
Macbeth!
Macbeth doth beseech me, my thoughts span these warm sacred waters
I must wear my armour and foresee the redundant prophecies, Duncan's
Body must rise to the high alters,
May this man's puzzle be put at final ease.
'Coming dearest!'

Idabel Mercy Chimsuku (17)

Days Of Not Making Plays

William Shakespeare is known for his array of plays,
But what did he do on the days he was not making plays?
Would he walk around in a daze,
Head in the clouds, thoughts lost in a maze?
Was he sunbathing at bays,
Or creating a phrase?
Who knows what William did on the days he was not making plays?

Did he fill out surveys,
Helping students with essays?
Did he eat food at buffets,
Or dine at cafés?
Who knows what William did on the days he was not making plays?

Could he cook bolognese,
Soak up sun's rays?
Is there a person he obeys,
Or did he set wood ablaze?
Who knows what William did on the days he was not making plays?

Molly Emery

O My Love

O Juliet
Why do thou look so sad
When the stars bow down to you as you smile
Your beauty gazes like the almighty sun
And I see diamonds in the centre of your eyes
They shine so bright
Just like you
My love
My all
My one
Who makes all my troubles vanish like
The sun at dusk
Your presence warms me
So greatly
O my sweet, sweet love
Must you
Leave
Me.

Asha Sutton (16)

The Tempest

A duke of Milan
Who had forcefully gone,
Pushed out of his role
With his heart and soul,
His daughter Miranda
Who had a lovely temper,
He found an island
Where he raised a diamond
And adopted two servants
Who helped with events,
He practised his magic
Until one day something tragic,
His enemies washed up on the shore,
Right into Prospero's core,
The king's son fell in love with Prospero's daughter,
Their hearts were out of order,
Prospero punished and pestered
The kings, dukes and jesters,
All was fine at the end
When they were forgiven and treated as a friend,
Prospero once again was the Duke of Milan,
And everyone was happy and so on.

Charlotte Hickey

Romeo And Juliet

Two star-crossed lovers, allocated from two enemy families,
their decades of hostility finally reach to tragedies.

This love is so strong and deep, that marriage is embarked in secret,
it brings a ray of hope to change and true regret.

Obstacles who are confrontational and combative are removed from the
path,
however, the lovers have to still face the city's wrath.

Fate departs Juliet's consort,
there's no escape but death, announces court.

Destiny plays yet another game,
to wed Juliet to another's name.
To Romeo it brings great shame!

Paris is the name of this fellow man,
but him and his world cannot break the span.

This apparent death brings significant shock,
to find their daughter dead is quite a knock.

In gratitude of their daughter, she is placed in a tomb,
little does Juliet know this will lead to Romeo's doom.

As the young man finds his wife 'dead',
due to a lack of knowledge delivered to his head,
he executes something which brings dread.

When Juliet awakes from her sleeping-beauty slumber,
she finds one less number.

To her heart's dismay,
there, her lifeless husband lay,
it was the ultimate sacrifice he was willing to pay.

Incomplete Juliet struck out a dagger and sighed out her last breath,
as this love story resulted in complete death.

Simran Akther Simmy (15)

Henry The Fifth

I sit here on my perch,
On my throne,
On the outside,
I am a lion,
I roar ferociously,
I am proud and fear is below thee,
But inside,
I feel weak,
My troubles and woes,
Feel beyond me,
They torment my soul,
Thy very first man was corrupted,
Any other was the same,
But some show it more than others,
And these French fools are a plain example,
I am their rightful king,
So stiffen the sinews my men,
Conjure the blood,
Stand like greyhounds in the slips,
For this weathered soul,
Will lead to a battle,
The battle of Agincourt.

Alice Annie Elizabeth Jackson

I, Lady Macbeth

Committed,
Though men tis proven I should fear -
I shall fight the coward 'till death do us part!'

Know that on the account of my craving,
It shall never bear the mind of I,
But my flesh - possessed.
Taken, by the late king.

For dedicated I shall ever remain,
My destiny shall be queen,
Therefore, my only desire will be so,
My only goal,
Hope,
Aim.
No fearful man shall I allow spite that.

A new age shall come,
A new deed completed,
All the laws men passed . . .
Lady Macbeth shall beat it.

Lauren Rachel Dinnall (14)

Bottom's Tail

Have you seen a man with furry ears?
He is a rather unattractive sight.
But, for him, Titania weeps her tears,
Where fairies dance underneath the bright light.
With a garland of flowers on his head,
He sings great songs over the moonlit lake.
'What angel wakes me from my flow'ry bed?'
Is what Titania asks when she does wake.
This strange love makes Puck, the small fairy, laugh.
As Oberon's mischief spreads all around
It wraps up the land like a silken scarf.
It's the character we've quite forgotten,
The donkey, once an actor, named Bottom.

Anna Elizabeth Grayson (11)

His Lifeline

Young little Shakespeare, a child of 1564, young little Shakespeare, he didn't know what was to come.
His story - or rather poem, started on 23rd April; a little baby boy,
Raised in Stratford-upon-Avon, with seven siblings, his dad and his mum,
Living a good life and a good education; but it wasn't all such a joy.

Young little Shakespeare wedded his wife, Anne Hathaway, in 1582 whom he adored and cared for,
Then came the baptism of Susanna Shakespeare - his first child, six months after.
His family grew - twins Hamnet and Judith were born, surely he didn't want any more?
His life became complete - full of love, happiness and laughter.

1592's young little Shakespeare - not so young, went to work in theatres and left his home,
So soon, he realised it's not all it appears to be; for him he couldn't choose - to be or not to be?
People in this world can be so cruel . . . Young little Shakespeare had never felt so alone.
But maybe there was hope, when The Globe Theatre was born. Was it his 'to be' key?

So let's skip a few years ahead, after a few visits of royalty, his son's death
And several long years of sonnet after sonnet on stage, and even thirty-eight plays,
Young little William Shakespeare took his final performance, his final bow, and his final curtain in 1616.
His final hours and even more to come, we shall remember him . . . the greatest writer of all the days.

Lauren Middleton

Lady Macbeth

Oh isn't she cruel that Lady Macbeth
She bosses people about which are bad
She kills a lot and won't stop at one death
She is so bad she drove her husband mad.

She does not care, she would kill a baby
She knows loads of potions that make you twitch
She really is not a normal lady
She could be a really bad cursing witch.

But everyone thinks she's a lady
But that is really wrong on all accounts
But to be known she would have a baby
Even if there were too many to count.

So Lady Macbeth she is not normal
And definitely not very formal.

Carenza Johnstone (13)

My Love Bloomed In Paradise

Juliet woke up with a panic-stricken heart.
Where is my love?
Where is my star-crossed love?
The wings of night swooped past spreading sadness in her heart.
My relationship with Romeo dissolved like the life of a human's death.
Where is my love?
Where is my star-crossed love?
The start of my love was a dream but the end of my love is art.
My beautiful tyrant is the same as a powerful weapon.
The ruthless weapon killed my dear Romeo.
Where is my love?
Where is my star-crossed love?
My heart jiggled with a discountable tune that made me dejected.
God set our love in paradise.
We both find a new, relaxing home.
Now, I've found my love.
I've found my star-crossed love!

Tharani Maheswaran (9)

The Difference

One troubled girl
One unseen boy
Two worlds collide,
On the inside
No one believes that what they have is real,
But how can one believe when one cannot feel
The difference, in the air,
When the two are near
Each other, hearts beating as one.
So listen to this twisted tale,
One that will surely turn you all pale,
It shall leave you doubting what is and is not real,
Unless you can feel,
The difference.

Sabah Athar

William Shakespeare

On April 23rd it all began
With seven sisters and brothers
Mary Shakespeare was his mother
Also, John was his father.
The powerful Stratford-upon-Avon man
That wrote like no other
Made Anne Hathaway his lover.
His lovely wife Anne
Married him aged twenty-six
Giving him three children
Whilst living in a house made of sticks.
Living through the Black Death
Hamnet's condition was something they couldn't fix
On the 23rd of April 1616, he took his last breath.

Kelly Dixon (13)

Shakespeare's Sonnet

O, Shakespeare,
O, Shakespeare,
O, how we miss thee!
Thy words wast magic,
Blessed by the gods.
Thee spun them like straw,
With such ease.
Hamlet, Othello and Macbeth;
All dark poetic verses laced with blood,
Making even the strongest cower!
As hard as they might try,
The amateurs today, as hard as they might try
Will never be you.
O, for you are the great Shakespeare!

Sarah Nazir (12)

Macbeth

A trio of misleading illusions,
preparing to plant a seed,
their influence, an instrument
that landed in the hands of Macbeth.

As his teachers,
they provided the music,
the first notes to a sinister melody,
ending in a catastrophe named death.

His lady encouraged his passion,
helping to pluck his strings,
she watered it.
Her motivation, a shower of nutrients,
for his sweet music.
Not that she knew.

As magic grew wildly,
evil unveiled,
the dark side no longer a shadow.

An overconfident young man,
exposed to the conflict,
between man and the supernatural.

Death became sealed,
love became scars.
All for his own greed.

A whirlwind exploded,
in his mind,
as a trio of shadows,
faded into the set of sun.

Megan McIntosh (16)

Romeo And Juliet

In the very beautiful land of Stratford,
Two noble families in rivalry,
Both families prepared to shed their blood,
From ancient hatred to present jealousy,
Two lovebirds take their life in agony,
Sadly true lovers decide to break free,
Seems like a misfortunate fantasy,
They fight for freedom and sadly agree,
To commit suicide together,
We will watch this for the next two hours and,
See their doomed love become a poor failure,
Their unfortunate deaths put an end,
To the everlasting family feud,
Which nothing but the children's deaths could subdue.

Sharukaa Uthayasekaran

Shakespeare - Golden Brick Wall

Once upon a time, a legend was born
That would change the way we think about dawn,
The blissful night sky like a thick blanket,
Nor could the heavens even peep through it,
He changed the ways we called entertainment,
Told us a story through only pen and parchment,
With such richness in his every word,
No wonder his messages were quickly heard,
Techniques that we are discovering today,
The graciousness of this language just can't be thrown away,
Appreciation on many different grades,
Analysing it like atoms, many shapes and many shades,
Interpretations, opinions and views galore,
There is no room to just focus on the plot any more.
Shakespeare said that the world is a stage
And he inspired me to make the world a better place.
If you focus too hard when the obvious is gone,
You can express your feelings throughout a song.
Emotions, facial expressions, body language,
As humans we are entitled to them all,
But it's also about building morals,
Think of your morals as a brick wall.
You start off with one brick, and as time goes on you finally build a wall,
But without the hard work, no plan and foundations, it will certainly be
doomed to fall.
Such as in Macbeth, nothing good is in for the bad,
But with that being said,
You should rather want to be glad than be sad,
Shakespeare was a cunning man,
His genius still amazes us all,
So listen to his words and learn from your mistakes,
Build your own golden brick wall.

Jasmine Hoque (13)

The Helpless Night

She would cry as she struggled to sleep.
She craved love, like the ocean, so daring and deep.
She would look at the dark and dying sky.
Mesmerised on the true beauty of high.

She would look at her only friend.
Reassure herself, she would be there, in the end.
She would look at the dying star.
Knowing how she felt, the beautiful scar.

Stars are broken and yet they shine
She knew that sadly that was not her line
She knew where she belonged truly,
Life had to be so surely.
She wanted to run, wanted to disappear,
With the stars, she shall be, but she was still here.
She knew what had to be done,
To make sadness disappear, pain run
She took the object, put it to her heart.
And she knew it wouldn't hurt, not at the start.

As her tear rolled down her chin,
She smiled at the window, she grinned.
She pulled the trigger, not knowing what she had done.
And with that last tear, she was gone.

Arlina Hysenaj (15)

Dearest Ophelia

What doest one see? A single quaint rose floating amid the still, sombre water.
With the eldritch voices the lady sleeps,
As the creation surrounding her sighs and weeps.
Shalt the brook and its tides nev'r awake her,
For this world is greatly complex to an innocent stranger.

A young lady once deranged by ardent love,
Now a mere soul that glides peacefully through the wind like a prepossessing dove.
For one's love never fades, even in death those pale white hands still clutch a single sprig of rosemary.

With the spectres trailing her lifeless body deeper,
Another mortal selleth their soul to the reaper.
A fair maiden so unpretentious and naive,
Sinking gradually, leaving mankind to mourn, to grieve.

As the ill-starred maiden is laid to rest,
Leaves of rue are placed on her motionless chest.

Amina Ara (16)

Foolish Macbeth

Oh foolish Macbeth, oh silly Macbeth,
You know not what you've done,
Now you're lying in the ground,
Remembering battles you haven't won.

Macbeth was a grand gentleman,
Living in the now,
Where did it all go wrong for him?
That's what I'll tell you now.

Macbeth rode his horse like a true soldier should,
He sat up high and proud,
Not knowing that in future he would,
Be tempted to steal the crown.

Three witches tempted him with fate,
He now wishes he'd never known,
They told him to take someone else's life,
But instead he condemned his own.

Macbeth made a stupid mistake,
He killed a man with trust,
Now he is threatened by many,
Because of his power lust.

Perhaps if he'd not been a fool,
If he hadn't called the bluff,
He may have survived through the battle,
And not been killed by Macduff.

Oh foolish Macbeth, oh silly Macbeth,
You can't undo your sin,
Now you're lying in the ground,
Remembering battles you'll never win.

Eva Stewart (15)

She, Macbeth

Bound by femininity, the cruellest cage.
I sought to find the words that a woman's lips could speak
I needed a man's -

A man's mouth to spew the foulness,
the darkness, the fire.
My breasts do not allow.

Lips too pink, too soft
to utter what my furious mind yearns to shriek.
Hands too small to lift the knife that slits the throats of the weak.

The dragon in my chest fumes,
claws at my throat to be released.
'Away, tendrils of expectation! Of branding and of - man!'
Mater. Terra. Ventris.

Conor Kirwan (16)

The Life Of Shakespeare - Bard Of Avon

Shakespeare, Shakespeare, still in our hearts
Teacher, preacher, how do you write so much,
Each and every piece strikes like a dart
You possess qualities that a human's brain would crunch
Such an intricate rhyme scheme
Hamlet, Macbeth, too many to count
So many plays, an arsenal that portrays your dreams,
Characters that encounter, pursue, the list mounts,
However it is too good to be true,
You also have tragedies,
You gifted your wife a second-hand bed, as bad as the flu,
Your tragedies are no remedies,
Unlike sweet candies,
Your tragedies are bitter just like my letter!

Mahee Ifthekhar Rohim (12)

Love At First Sights

L ove struck the two hearts of Romeo and Juliet
O h, how they loved one another, if they could be with each other
V iolence struck before with the death of Tylbalt (Juliet's cousin)
E very blood that dropped from Tylbalt was a lifetime of Romeo
   being banished from the city.

A rranged marriage upon Juliet to Paris though she was secretly married
T he plan had been formed by the friar with Juliet pretending to be dead,
   however Romeo wasn't informed about this.

S hocking news reached Romeo of Juliet's death so he sped back
   to the city, back to her grave
I nside lay Juliet plagued by a sleeping drug,
   making her have the mask of death
G ingerly the tomb door opened with Romeo behind it
H aving found Juliet dead, Romeo committed suicide
T hen Juliet awoke and found Romeo dead
   and killed herself using Romeo's sword
S o together they lay dead, 'For never was a story of more woe
   than this of Juliet and her Romeo.'

Abisóla Abdul-Obitáyo (11)

23

Existence

He is ruthless and unmerciful yet is reliable and selfless
He is a man's best friend and his support is endless
Yet turns out to be his greatest foe till your last breath
He can be the reason for survival as well as the cause of death
He bring hopefulness and brightness clearing all dust
Yet creates an atmosphere of darkness, doubt and distrust

He mounts beyond all hopes, a bastion of invincibility, he has fortitude and determination
He can help yet hinder your chances of survival for he is a man's greatest affiliation
No him, no life as he is valuable, valid and versatile
He is meant to facilitate your survival and make you smile
He is there for your assistance and to show persistence
Yet he is ignored so hard he begins to doubt his own existence

He is like rainfall falling from the sky
He helps provide life for those living life so dry
He extinguishes your wishes and shows you harsh reality
He gets rid of all that filth in your mentality
Recognition that he is essential is disrespected
People go on in life while his mind is getting infected

Who can deny him as he defies all obstruction?
Without him you are doomed for destruction
If he likes it he shall keep it close to his heart and it shall bind
With him yet, if he doesn't he won't let it even wander near his mind
He can help you but he is not sought or needed for that is hopeless
He is not weak and his presence is invaluable but his being is pointless

He is silenced, ignored and not acknowledged, his confidence is shattered and damaged
Causing him to think if he really exists? He no longer has the courage to persist
To be, or not to be: that is the question
But the answer to that question lies in yet another question
If he listens to his heart, it is definitely there.
But If he listens to his mind, certainly it is not there
Should he take a life, or give his own life
Should he remain, or should he not . . .

His passion could be the reason for your existence
And your victory could be a result of your persistence
He owes us very little but we owe it everything
Yet he is treated like he is nothing
His existence is thought permanent
However his end will be determinant
There is nothing good or bad
It is our existence which makes it so.

Salman Ibrahim Uddin (16)

Macbeth's Medicine

Victory! comes together like a couple's embrace,
Fought without thinking, winning lights up your face,
A letter sent to our lady holding emotions fit to burst,
She knows that from you, she can't expect the worst.

You are twisted and perceived the complete wrong way,
King Duncan's right-hand man has made a mistake,
Thane of Glamis gets an honourable mention,
Titles promised, witches prophesied great tension,
After Thane of Cawdor, be brave and stand up:
King of Scotland until the people have had enough.

Tell your lady and let her whisper sweet nothings,
Preys on you because you are vulnerable, trusting.
Because of disloyalty and lack of faith,
Getting without receiving, give without take,
Cawdor shall live though he is another,
One shall die due to the father,
Of Scotland, and ominous bells will ring,
Remember what happens when you mess with the king.

Twisting your little finger, serpent in your ear,
Deceives your conscience, invites it to her lair.
Abhor her slithering words, she is not absolute,
She will become insane and you a merciless brute.
Your other half should have been pensive about you,
Instead she calculated her options and wrung out the truth.

Love is blind, but she knows desire is crystal-clear,
Like peppered moths in the night, openings shall appear.
Pivot, make a U-turn, your heart in your eyes,
This love is a fiend - a growing complex web of lies.
Macbeth, what better way to welcome your guest?
Than giving him a room with a comfortable bed,
To lie in, after a successful banquet, a dance with a beat,
Then creep in like an imposter and kill him in his sleep?

The wish to feel better once the deed is done,
The only thing stronger than sin that has begun.
Your soul is unclean and your aura deep red,
A noble man killed unconscious in his bed.

Clean the knives and cleanse your hands,
Go back to bed until the change of the hands,
Pretend you know little, lady, nothing at most,
Scream, cry and faint like an innocent host.
The witches are reminding Macbeth in his mind,
You've lost it now, though this is your time.

Right or wrong as the coin may land,
There is no denying the fate of your hand.
Run your fingers down your wife's arm,
Kid yourself that you will keep her from harm.
She has already thrust herself in this mess,
See what happens when greed doesn't rest.

Your lady has always been a delicate flower,
Don't blame yourself for the past hour,
Her influence was great, your love delusional,
On point now, before we hear of your funeral.

Ravens, crows, grave sites and black cats,
Death is what it is - you can't change that,
No turning back time for crime hath been committed,
And Banquo suspects thou is the foul criminal.

Although the clock can't be brought back,
You can bargain with God and work off your own back,
The choice is only yours, you can make it,
Your life has always been yours, can you take it?
Macbeth the great, an imposter in the king's feet,
Take off the robe, your riches are sickening,
You have no right to scare the brothers Malcolm and Donalbain,
I never thought I'd live to see the day when you changed.

Spawn of the Devil, spinner of black gold,
Listen to the witches, and do what you're told.
The time is ticking, your wife sees things no longer there,
Your empathy thin, and your goodness running bare.
I look forward to the day when you are tested and tried,
With some luck, they'll hang you and skin your hide.

Ah ha! Banquo's sons will inherit your throne,
How can this be when you stand alone?
Attempt to get rid of your friend Banquo and his son,
Three murderers couldn't hide that you were the one.
Fleance escapes from your ruthless wrath,
Banquo's spirit visits you - he has to come back.

At a feast you only see red,
Even your wife can't make amends,
Admit that this once your wits are lost,
You are stuck in the present, this is the cost.

Go back to the witches as you have done before,
You are scared, frightened, you beg, you implore.
You won't be killed by a man woman-born,
Your heart so cold, while the weather so warm.
But, you know the answer, you can fix this:
Kill Macduff's wife, seize his home, kill his children.

Macbeth the authoritarian still lives on,
Though when Birnham Wood is seen it won't take long.
The brothers have returned, their revenge sickly sweet,
Though you had an army and castle, you are now dead meat.

Malcolm, King of Scotland, the crown is rightfully yours at Scone,
Macduff has finally given Macbeth a deserving taste of his own.

Nicola-Mary Geraghty (16)

Romeo Thought He Saw Juliet Stir

The cold glass bottle lay before me,
a fitting end for a twisted character.
The cord of love entangled me,
slowly throttling the tears
from glazed-over eyes.
She lay there,
not so pale as she should be;
elegant nightdress floating across
her sunlit skin.
A loud cry of frustration escaped from between cracked lips.
Thought I saw her stir. . .
no couldn't be.
Cried out to the heavens for mercy -
a plea for help from an unpleasant soul.
Gnarled talons grabbed hold of the torture;
trembling fingers unscrewed it.
Maybe it was the way it smelt; sweet white wine
on a snowflaked day -
pure water cleansing a chapped stomach.
Shut those irises and downed it in one.
Burning breath
came upon me; knocked down
my organ's systems and
took control of the beating of my heart.
Or lack, thereof.
Maybe I should've waited.
Waited for the timing of God.
Couldn't feel as I slumped
against her flushed,
warm skin.
Couldn't feel.
'Romeo? Is that you?'

Opefoluwa Sarah Adegbite (13)

Shakespeare Acrostic Poem

S hakespeare is one of the world's greatest writers who wrote plays
 and poetry
H amlet has a mixture of personalities rolled into one including
 aggression and passiveness
A ntony and Cleopatra's story is a tragedy about love
K ing Lear descends into madness after bitter battles
 with his youngest daughter
E dmund is the Earl of Gloucester's illegitimate son
S hylock is a Venetian moneylender from Verona in
 'The Merchant of Venice'
P etruchio is a gentleman from Verona in 'The Taming of the Shrew'
E dgar is heir to the Earl of Gloucester
'A s You Like It' is based on the medieval story of Rosalynde
 by Thomas Lodge
R ichard III was Shakespeare's most successful play
E arl of Gloucester is King Lear's oldest friend and ally.

Nidhi Joshi (9)

Face Your Difficulties

In life there are many difficulties
Although it's hard you still have to face these
Brighten up your mood by eating ice cream
You can feel the excitement in the breeze
Did you know happiness lies everywhere?
Then after this feed the hungry bear
If you're bored then read a fantastic book
If there's difficulties then don't be sad
Try to keep your very beautiful smile
If you're unhappy then it's very bad
Go, feel free and run a very long mile
If you're bored and want something to hear
Then you hear poems from the great Shakespeare.

Rayhan Ahmed (11)

My Love

My love? Yet if my eyes do not deceive me you are far from it.
For once I awoke and my eyes came to rest on a maiden as fair as the summer morn
Yet now I again rise but now verily I do see a witch, a hag!
Truly, it is not the beauty for your fairness is more than that of all the land,
Instead your virtues.
Oh gone are they, where are they gone?
Has my summer morn become a bitter winter night?
You sting with your words, your tongue that of a snake,
You beat those who help and scold those who teach.
Truly you devour all joy that first resided in your beating heart.

My love? Is it you? I cry to say it is and now thou art bitter as the storm and vile as an asp.
Alas, my love is gone, and so I long to flee too.

Jyothi Cross (13)

Shakespeare Rocks!

Shakespeare had a talent, no other poet could balance.
'Midsummer's Night Dream' was a lovely scheme,
'The Taming of the Shrew' was really quite new.
'Romeo and Juliet' were the perfect duet
Though Montague and Capulet did not think they were a matching set.

Shakespeare was the best, he never took a rest.
Beatrice and Benedick made 'Much Ado About Nothing',
And Hamlet made Denmark rotten.
Malcolm and Donalbain were to bear the blame
But Macduff killed Macbeth and that was enough.

Shakespeare's writing is exciting.
'The Tempest' is the bestest,
Wizards, magic, storms and thorns.
I'm no fan of Caliban
But Miranda is kind(a)... and Shakespeare Rocks!

Isabel Jackson (10)

Romeo And Juliet

Inside the brick walls of the tomb
A blossoming love was doomed
Because of a lot of family hatred
Romeo and Juliet lay stone dead
No more of Romeo with his soft curls
No more of Juliet with eyes like pearls
Both lay drenched in scarlet blood
As red as Red Riding Hood's hood
The moonlight by their death was shattered
And the tomb walls were blood-splattered
Their families wept tears like wild rain
For out of their feud two lovers were slain
But away from storms of death and greed
Where selfish villains never succeed
Where the rainbows of good are high above
Romeo and Juliet have eternal love.

Shaona Mitra

Juliet's Confession

Romeo, Romeo did you love *me,* Romeo?
Was Rosaline not your heart's desire?
Before your hungry eyes found me
Star-crossed lovers, a story of our destruction.

A rose by any other name would smell as sweet
And yet only the scent of a rose could stir your heart
A Capulet rose, for Rosaline bore this ancient name too
The forbidden fruit tastes the sweetest on youthful lips.

Two houses, unalike by our own admission
Yet so familiar, by more than our dignity
Montague, was it I that you loved
Or the zeal of plucking a rose from your foe's garden?

Civil war and our unclean hands
Tearing fair Verona apart with word driven blades
Did our youthful minds betray us?
We traded our lives for a kiss from the enemy.

Romeo, Romeo did I love *you*, Romeo?
My childish dreams of a handsome prince
Came in the form of a Montague
Our criminalised love, excitement for the young.

Was our death all for naught?
A juvenile love that would fade with time
Yet our families put there archaic dispute aside
My father and Montague, so full of woe
All caused by my crush on Romeo.

Katie Lee-Kearns (17)

Shakespeare's Play Inspirational!

No one trusted when Romeo and Juliet came,
The sky turned blue with stars to make the feeling of love immersing in life.
Nothing was believed and felt till the feeling of romance,
The shyness of Juliet and Romeo and the sudden meeting changed the destiny.
The play Romeo and Juliet put an end to hatred and more steps to love.
True love was not believed and was easy to be broken,
Suddenly Romeo and Juliet gave a belief that love is keen and cannot break.
The sudden twist of the play Romeo and Juliet brought happiness but sadness
When no one trusted it at the end.
The play gave a role model of everyday life of a strong love that can never be broken.
Trust your love.

Namra Durrani (13)

Swim!

You may not appreciate the nibbling fishes;
the sand-covered sandwiches eaten on beaches,
these are not things that anyone wishes -
the terrible screeches when knocking off leeches.

You also say you hate the local pool,
the cringing chlorine and the extreme deeps
and the sky-high diving board so tall
and the strange cloudy dust which gathers in heaps.

But I'm telling you you've got to take the leap,
dive into the water and swim like a shark,
you'll be energised by the starting beep,
it's tremendous, a truly great lark.

So make sure you go to your local pool,
it's extremely good fun and extremely cool!

Joe Parker (12)

Ps I Lear You: Confessions Of An Old King

A tragic hero I am,
Do I give a damn?
My head is quite long gone,
Since I last gave up my throne.
Daughters to choke Cinderella's sisters a wince,
A losing battle with myself long since.
A corrupted royal court,
Has left me fallen short.
A fool smarter than I, do I possess.
My dear Cordelia who loves me,
Pretty flower, no more, no less.

Then loyal Kent,
Always at the scene.
A Lady Lear? Oh Countess Gloucester?
No queen?
No help have I, a confused ol' guy
Out of house, out of home
The Heath so I did roam.
With flowers in my snow-white beard,
I realised all my folly
And feared. (Though I looked quite weird).

For the wrongs I did to a kingdom so faded,
As the tender daisies and weeds I jaded.
A head not fit to hold a crown,
Adieu dear friends;
Such tragedy it is, when a king's the real clown.

Katie Bell (18)

William Wrote Sonnets

William wrote sonnets. The best in the world ever.
William was born in Stafford-upon-Avon
William Shakespeare was very, very clever
Shakespeare never wrote with any crayon
William shall be remembered as a hero
William's master of Romeo and Juliet
Shakespeare would never write with a biro
Shakespeare loved writing in couplets
William wrote in couplets for his sonnets
Without Shakespeare yonder will be no light
William Shakespeare is very true and honest
William Shakespeare was always very right
Shakespeare plays were for entertainment
Shakespeare never had an arraignment.

Melisa Ak (12)

Rosaline

Rosaline's cheeks are red as roses,
Her eyes as blue as the sky.
Her teeth are white as a pearl,
Oh Rosaline, my love.

Rosaline's dress is green as grass,
It sparkles like dewdrops in the sun.
Her shoes are wavy as the water,
Oh Rosaline, my love.

Rosaline's garden is bright as sun,
Jasmine's on the wall.
I love you Rosaline,
Oh Rosaline, my love.

Hana Strelcova (8)

Juliet, My Love

I was intoxicated by her touch,
The way she twisted her hair
And how every breath was a
Sacrifice by the forgivable air.

I gently kissed her lips,
Like I was drowning and she
Was the only thing that could
Ever save me.

Thee Juliet, my love,
Shining brighter than thee sun,
In thee sky above.

O God, please help me now,
Let Juliet be with me,
Somehow.

Juliet my love,
Where are you now
Up in thee sky
And not in the ground.

I shall not live
Without you by my side,
So off I go, into Heaven I glide.

Juliet my love,
We can be together now,
For together we shall be happy again.

Juliet my love,
Without you I am drowning
And I cannot breathe.

Lydia Smith (15)

Shall I Compare Love

Shall I compare love to a steaming train?
Here to catch but gone before one hath time to think.
Shall I ride upon her teasing wonder
And risk one's heart to be brutally crushed?
Will I end upon the lonely platform
Riding these rails 'til all love is dead?
Or shall one just wait for the next passing ride?
Waiting and watching for love to find I?

What if my ticket is not right for me
And one is left standing waiting for thee?

Karen Lagan (13)

My Shakespearean Sonnet

Two lovers; Capulet and Montague
They were torn apart by an endless feud
Juliet, if only he could see you
And Romeo's family, oh so rude.
The two lovers danced freely at a ball
Tybalt saw them and enraged drew his sword,
'Back down my son, with him she'll never fall,'
Spoke Tybalt's father, the high, mighty lord.
A vile liquid caused Juliet's fake death
News came to Romeo, he was distraught
He got to her tomb; he took one last breath,
His lover Juliet thought her last thought.
Along the tomb floor blood started to rain,
Both families' lives filled with endless pain.

Charlie Williams (11)

Willm Shaksp . . . Or William Shakespe . . . Or Wm Shakspe . . . Or William Shakspere?

William Shakespeare is an anagram you see
For 'I am a weakish speller', hee hee
Signing his name
Was never the same
With 80 variations, he never spelt it correctly!

But he did write books you know,
Because stories used to flow
From his head to his toes
Like a tap waterflow.

Romance, intriuge, murder you have it all
Mr Shakespeare was a know-it-all.

Ishan Chattopadhaya (11)
Bacon's College, London

Romeo

If Romeo and Rosaline were a happening thing
The Bard's story might have had a happier ending
But Juliet appeared
And as was feared
His second choice proved a fatal thing.

Cyril Kweku Torsu (13)
Bacon's College, London

Wedding Day

Guests receive an invitation by mail
Spreading the news and wrapping up presents
Packing essentials and bottles of ale
Hoping that their day shall be quite pleasant.

The bride thinking about what might go wrong
The bridesmaids calming her down as she cries
Walking down the aisle to an orchestral song
Knowing the fact she'll be loved when she dies.

A promise made never to be broken
A trusting partnership sealed with a ring
The truth as promised has to be spoken
People admire the bride's dress of bling
And there on the church pews sits a small dove
Simply there to show the symbol of love.

Claire Johnston (13)
Beeslack High School, Penicuik

Remembering

When we sit for seconds, we can sit for days
Remembering the times we spent together
The road will split into two ways
And I will go into fairer weather.

As I sit beside your bed
My mind goes back to our time in the sea
And is filled with horrible dread
As I remember the pain you saw with me.

But as I sit I feel the hate
Come rushing up to meet the truth
I suddenly feel a heavy weight
As I remember you died in youth.

I realise I have been blind
Months and years are now behind.

Douglas Perry (14)
Beeslack High School, Penicuik

Promise

A promise between lovers to protect
A decision to make it official
An act to prove promises can be kept
Marriage can be seen as successful
Although worth the pain for people in love
It is a huge step in a couple's life
Sometimes symbolised by a white dove
A husband now has a beautiful wife
It's for those who love each other the most
The precious ring slipped onto the finger
You cannot miss the emotional toast
After the wedding the feeling lingers
Who will fall in love next? Who will be brave?
Who will let love take over and be saved?

Laura Yapp (13)
Beeslack High School, Penicuik

Loveless Life

I'm trapped in a cage,
Never knowing if I am going to be set free.
It's like freezing in the Ice Age,
I feel like I'm getting swept out to sea.
Often I think of you,
Your eyes put the stars to shame,
If only you knew.
Your love is like a burning flame,
But as I sit here waiting for your love,
You have found another,
As you fly away gracefully like a dove
We will never find one another,
So long as the sun burns bright
I will never let you out of my mind's sight.

Jennifer Watt (13)
Beeslack High School, Penicuik

Flower

Little seed very tiny and so small
When it started it looked quite like a bean
Will sometime in its life become so tall
One day in its life the stem will turn green
This small, tiny, green thing will make you think
It will make you think about its power
What colour will it turn - orange or pink?
All of these things are about a flower!
This flower will probably be pretty
The middle of the flower has pollen
The colour and scent will attract a bee
In autumn the petals will start falling
Flowers are pretty and wonderful things
Flowers are Mother Nature's diamond rings!

Lucy Black (14)
Beeslack High School, Penicuik

Passing

When I was small time was covered by youth
Endless holidays were given to play
Nothing I cared in my childhood for truth
Or for time slipping silently away
Pages of pictures, grandparents able
This book I see holds both present and past
Faces smile around a summer's table
Surely, we thought, these moments all would last
But I should live in the here and the now
Making every word, thought and action count
For I am only here as time allows
Time can't be relived and the minutes mount
Oh, how our moments quickly reach their end
What can we do to challenge and contend?

Hew Murray (13)
Beeslack High School, Penicuik

Marriage

A promise made, never to be broken,
Two hearts bound together, officially.
Represented by a ring, a token
Vows describe two people's love vividly.
A beautiful bride with red, rosy cheeks
And a groom in a suit, handsome and broad.
Planning the wedding for weeks upon weeks
Soon to venture on honeymoon abroad.
Forever together, where they belong,
Till death do them part, the minister said.
Walk down the aisle to orchestral song,
Together again, the dance the groom led.
Be with each other forever they may,
The start of the rest of their lives this day.

Jodie Claire McCarlie (14)
Beeslack High School, Penicuik

The Beauty Of Nature

How fast these minutes flow into an hour,
As each year passes the pace increases.
Reducing time to see sun, cloud or flower.
Going so quickly, soon our time ceases,
To revel in the beauty of our world.
The sun on our skin, the wind in our hair.
As summer comes the petals are unfurled.
Wandering the shoreline without a care.
The colours of the sunset every night,
The softness of the duckling, the swaying of the tree.
Such elegance will always bring delight.
These priceless gifts available to all for free.
Please make sure to plan, as the years go by,
To appreciate nature, as time will fly.

Hollie Fullerton (13)
Beeslack High School, Penicuik

Hourglass

A second quickly becomes a minute
Your life slowly draining away
Russian roulette, just let go of the bullet
The 23 hours becoming a day
Birth, childhood, adulthood, death
Generation to generation passing on traditions
In and out just keep breathing
Fighting for your loved ones on your own mission
Each part of your body slowly giving up
All your life becoming memories
Never giving up
Loving, eventually going to marry
Going through your life
Watching it become rife.

Amy McQuillan (13)
Beeslack High School, Penicuik

Time Passing Sonnet

It can't be controlled, it cannot be stopped,
No matter how much we try hard to stay,
The secret of time is forever locked,
The logic may be discovered one day.

A second, a minute, hour or a day,
Moments we treasure gone in a click,
Who controls time, who takes it away?
Things we remember gone in a tick.

People we hold close become strangers,
Strangers we just met become closest friends,
Things we never could imagine happen,
New dreams come alive, old problems can mend.
Time is not unlimited, there will be an end,
Respect Father Time, make him your friend.

Emma Hedley (13)
Beeslack High School, Penicuik

Titania's Lullaby

You spotted ladybug with noble song,
Giant centipedes, be not seen,
Spotted snakes and furry legs, do no wrong,
Come not near our lovely queen.

Nectar and melody
Sing sweetly tonight;
Lulla, lulla, lullaby - lulla, lullaby.

Never harm
No nightmare, no horror,
Don't come to our fairy queen,
Lulla, lulla, lullaby - lulla, lullaby.

Silky spiders, come not near,
Soft snakes do not come,
We will sing a lullaby,
Lullaby, lullaby, lullaby.`

Libby Barron (8)
Benedict Biscop CE Academy, Sunderland

Titania's Lullaby

You spotted snakes with double tongues be not seen,
Thorny hedgehogs and blind worms
Never come near our fairy queen.

Philomel, with melody
Sing in our sweet lullaby,
Lulla, lulla, lullaby - lulla, lullaby.

Weaving spiders be not seen,
Do not come near our fairy queen.
Spotted hedgehogs so disgusting
Make them go away.

Never harm, nor spell, nor charm,
Come out lovely lady high;
Lulla, lulla, lulaby - lulla, lullaby.

Jasmine Gray
Benedict Biscop CE Academy, Sunderland

Titania's Lullaby

You mad hearted ants and busy bees
I thought you made honey,
Better get started!
You simpering snakes that slither away
Come not near our fairy queen I do pray.

Let our fairy queen sleep,
Lullaby, lullaby la,
Lullaby, lullaby, la,
Go to sleep,
Do not peek, we will protect you.

Let the queen sleep,
Let her have a dream,
Now let her be,
Go away because you are no bigger than a pea.

Let our fairy queen sleep,
Lullaby, lullaby, la,
Lullaby, lullaby, la,
Go to sleep,
Do not peek, we will protect you.

Go away and then you say
At the end of the day
Our fairy queen is sleeping,
She is having a dream,
Closer she gleams,
Lullaby, lullaby.

Neve Mullen
Benedict Biscop CE Academy, Sunderland

Titania's Lullaby

Thorny hedgehogs do no wrong
Slithering snakes are very long
Come not near our fairy queen
These nasty animals are not human beings

But go to sleep now
Thou scurvy iron-witted art our fairy queen
So animals be not seen

Then abominable, lily-livered
Fancy monger go away now
Silky spiders stop somehow
You withered flies go away

Our queen does not harm
Because to King Oberon she is a charm
Let the queen have some rest
Because she is the best

Thou green, slimy lizards
You're as good as wizards
Thou decayed puppy-headed horse - drench
Go away while the queen sleeps in her flowery bed.

S L
Benedict Biscop CE Academy, Sunderland

Titania's Lullaby

Shallow cream face
Block be not near.
Double tongued pigs
Come not near our fairy queen.

Listen to the flower sing
Like a gold tea pot sing
And lulla lulla lullaby.

Never harm your charm
With a spear near our queen.

Sweet little hummingbird
Lulla lulla lulla lullaby.

C M
Benedict Biscop CE Academy, Sunderland

Titania's Lullaby

You horrible snake, do no wrong.
You newts, you're grass roots.
Come not near our fairy queen.

Sleep, sleep but don't go beep, beep.
Slimy worms do no wrong
Or you will be so long.

Thorny hedgehogs you are now seen.
Hence you scary snake.
Let our queen have some rest.

Our queen does no harm
Because King Oberon is a lovely charm.

Come our lovely lady nigh;
Lulla lulla lulla lullaby.
Do no spell to our fairy queen.

N H
Benedict Biscop CE Academy, Sunderland

Sonnet XIII

And then he drew his sword of loathe and greed
Thy stab brought me to knees thou evil bain
May hatred hence from my soul, do not feed
Though my broken heart is not under reign
Hither I wait, come, come foolish one
Clutching lover's heart and upon my horse
I shall see to it that what must be done
For my brother has taken foolish course
Bright pale moonlight illuminates thou path
Thou fails to catch what hides in the shadows
Stolen trust has summoned merciless wrath
Love so great but his heart as ice no one knows
Then as I strike his head tumbles to Hell
And soon my sword finds my own head as well.

Sophia U Okwaraji (13)
Birralee International School, Trondeim

Sonnet CMXII

Shall I compare thee to my dearest book?
Thy lines and curses are more quaintly written.
Thou make thy reader sink into your look,
They try to leave but they have been smitten.

Thy writer is the author of this world,
He made it fast and spent his life on thou.

Thy pages are as precious as a pearl,
They make my soul soften, just with a bow.

To find a book like thou, I can search forever,
But one as fair as thou, is tough to find.

Fatima Naveed (13)
Birralee International School, Trondeim

Sonnet 9

I wondered once how thee became developed.
From men with sticks and sabre-toothed tigers.
Thee were primitive and undeveloped.
Now we have bikers, divers and lighters.

Before thee had to struggle to get fire.
Now we hath many lighters and firefighters.
We hath been inspired to build then retire.
Many wanted to become famous writers.

We no longer have sires or fancy town criers.
We have televisions where we watch survival.
That's unimportant, we just put food in the fryer.
Long time ago we had a big arrival.

We flew to the moon and we had a big sigher.
Now look at how much we through time did acquire.

Julian Veelo (13)
Birralee International School, Trondeim

Sonnet VIII

Thou art more precious than a flower bloom
I hopelessly wish I was dear to thee
I shall love thee even in my dark tomb
And no power on this Earth will stop me

So my dear beloved, please do not fret
Thee need nothing to improve anything
Thee have everything a girl longs to get
Maybe one day thou whilst accept my ring

Thou art too kindhearted to sweep me off
However thee do sweep me off my feet.
It feels so foul and thee deserve to scoff
For I'm thought of as nothing, but a cheat

Both my head and heart just lead me to thee
Now if only thee felt the same for me.

Natalia M Kirkebø-Redondo (13)
Birralee International School, Trondeim

The Seasons

Like a dog my tongue hangs out from my lips,
Without my water my throat is parched and dry.
My group of ecstatic friends buy chips
And eat them happily while time flies quickly by.

Like a tree's strong brown trunk I stand
Just staring at the sea of golden leaves;
A pretty scene of falling leaves to land
Soft comfy boots and long fluffy sleeves.

Like a log I stay stuck to the soft ground,
White blossom petals falling on my face.
The pink sunset is just like a candyfloss cloud,
The daffodils swaying at a consistent pace.

Hedy Clark (10)
Coopersale Hall School, Epping

A Sonnet On Time

The clock on my wall will tick until the night,
The picture on the wall will talk to me at day.
They really certainly give me a fright,
It only does it in the middle of May.
The time chops up my life into little chunks
The day divided into a problem sum,
The things I try I always seem to flunk.
The picture on the wall is shiny plums
To make me want to eat and not to die.
The clock ticks still and makes me mad,
I really might grow wings and learn to fly.
I am the very opposite of glad;
This is a very, very strange place
That has given me an angry, white face.

Jack Ronald Frederick Wilson (10)
Coopersale Hall School, Epping

Is Murder The Key?

Murderous thunder drums the blasted heath
Lightning splinters the bloodshot sky
Gnarled trees lurk, ensnaring unsuspecting victims
Cries from minions of death, echo across the moorland
Whilst stalking wind shackles weary travellers
Menacing portal of death
Invaded by darkness opens . . .

Inexplicably three malevolent crones emerge from the fog
Dressed in amorphous rags
Chappy fingers clasp hold of the heroes
Chanting twisted prophecies
Macbeth shall be king!
Time slows down, as dark thoughts grow
Will murder be the key to the future . . . ?

Chloë Green & Caira Tiana Forbes (10)

Great Chart Primary School, Ashford

Murderer

Forceful gales rage mightily
Guarding the secrets of the heath
Protecting the territory of the hags
Bringing grass to life
Electric veins burst through clouds
Reaching, reaching, reaching
For unfortunate victims
Eerie mists blanket the moons
Murdering the light.

Expanded space of dampness
Rocky death trap
Lonely
Mud
Murderer
Waiting
Ready to snatch away any life
That dares to grow
Lonely trees stand watching
Feeling, feeling, feeling
For poor innocent life
Sinister skeletons sit waiting
To stab the next victim
Evil lurking
Removing safety.

Old hags bent double
Weird sisters smothered in black
Gnarled
Waiting, waiting, waiting
For the one . . .

Anna Fitch (10)
Great Chart Primary School, Ashford

Death Side

Lightning lit the sky like stars
Thunder shook, dying earth
Driving rain lashed down
Wind howled like wolves
Fog swirled covering the living dead
Massive trees reached out
Jagged rocks are filled with darkness
Lightning like a tiger, ready to catch its prey

The cauldron bubbled
Wild looking witches assembled together
The storm swirled out of the cauldron
As black as the night sky
Searching, searching, searching
For the hidden light.

Ellie Louise Bellenie (11)
Great Chart Primary School, Ashford

Nightmare After Battle

Gnarled trees with skeletal fingers clutch at the soulless skies
Jagged rocks lurk like predators awaiting their prey
Whirling wind torments the mind
Now that the malevolent storm has awoken

Victorious warriors wander disorientated in a decimated moorland
Mist enshrouds a blind Macbeth
Clearing only to reveal three witches
Women with beards
Their unnaturally formed figures mirroring the trees
With ghostly voices echoing strange prophecies
Macbeth will be king

Lightning strikes, the hellish creatures are gone
Leaving the warriors' minds diseased
Will Macbeth go forward with his deep and darkest desires?

Bailey Robert Stevenson (11)
Great Chart Primary School, Ashford

Encountering Death

Skies fracture into millions of blood-stained pieces
Opening a malevolent portal of death
Gnarled, skeletal trees loom over the soulless heath
Grasping onto desperate, withering souls
Screeching, mocking winds torture their dying ears
While fog thicker than rivers blinds their useless eyes

Deformed, demented devils arrive from hell
Misplaced in a wonderful yet foul world not their own
Withered, snaking hair whips their deathly white skin
Ignored by the hunchback harbingers of death
Neither man nor woman, they dress in ancient, shredded robes
As their possessed voices carry like the wind itself

Shadows curl and silently consume the demons
Leaving nothing but their cracked, high-pitched voices
Mystical and confused, the two men carried on
While the storm's anger erupted around them
As they carried on their troublesome journey
They wondered if the hags' chant could ever come true.

Elizabeth Ollis (11)
Great Chart Primary School, Ashford

Mysterious Moor

Jagged rocks are minions of death on the corrupted wasteland
Gnarled trees stretch across the barren moor
Ferocious storm awakens from the misty sky
Eerie whispers haunt weary travellers casting unforgettable curses

Cackles of unearthly laughter of hideous hags appear
Chappy fingers beckon to come nearer
Hooked noses sniff the air for innocent flesh
Ragged hoods conceal their skeletal faces
Hairy beards forbid them to be women
A mutter of prophecies is spoken
'Thou shalt be king'
A spark of blinding smoke and they vanish
Lightning rashes through the air turning trees into ash
A demand of unanswered questions
Is all that remains of the vanished witches.

Harry Henshaw (11)
Great Chart Primary School, Ashford

Prophecies Foretold

Bruised skies scream as the devil's hand grazes the land
Skeleton trees reach out to greet the lightning
Growling like wolves the thunder awakes
Withered trees tower over passers-by
The grazed ground cracks as Macbeth marches through

As evil crows land
Blending into never-ending darkness
A sound like no other
Evil cackles fill Macbeth's frozen ears
Three fork lightning tears through the bruised skies
Three ugly crones with wild snaking hair
Like dead souls, as pale as ghosts, they sneak closer
Their words torment his ears
Prophecies spoken
Could they be true?

Jasmine Periam (11)
Great Chart Primary School, Ashford

Future Foretold

Malevolent masses of death tousle roughly,
Pacing shadows haunt the blasted heath
Skeletal fingers snatch through dense air.
A ghost's playground.
The barren lonely wastes of the moorland
Suffocate disorientated Macbeth.
Jagged rocks are death traps in this desolate place
Screeching gales of wind whip his cloak
He stumbles on blindly.

Serrated rocks inexplicably morph
Into dishevelled hags sent from the devil.
Hunched, shrivelled, deformed,
Murky, sunken eyes probe him.
Shrouded under the hoods of death.
Callused hands strain to touch him
Scarred, pearlescent faces, tangled knots of hair
Callused hands strain to touch him
'Hail Macbeth, who shall be king!'

Melting into the wind.
Gone.
Murder is left hanging in the air
As dark thoughts swirl in Macbeth's mind.

Ellie Wong (10)
Great Chart Primary School, Ashford

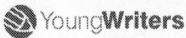
Destiny Awaits

The storm lurks in the cloud
Devious crows sing the song of death
Familiars of the unnatural
Unexpectedly lightning strikes, tearing moorland in half
Opening a never-ending portal of darkness
Twisted, gnarled trees stalk and loom over victorious men
Out of the gloom and fog, three rocks become ugly, withered and wild hags
They whisper unnatural prophecies, 'Thou shalt be king'
They invade the mortal world, filling Macbeth's mind with murderous thoughts
With a strike of lightning, they return to the underworld, leaving Macbeth to ponder.

Phoebe-Rose Hartshorne (11)

Great Chart Primary School, Ashford

Freaky Witches

Soulless sky awakened by thunder
Lightning strikes and lights up the lifeless tree
The blasted heath vibrates
Lurking rocks stare across the moorland

From three serrated rocks
Hags materialise to face Macbeth
With scruffy clothes, snaking hair
Flesh like skin
Lingering voices crackling peculiar things
Macbeth will be king

Lightning strikes as the witches vanish
Prophecies echo in the warriors' mind
Macbeth will be king.

Sam Harmer (10)
Great Chart Primary School, Ashford

Foretold Futures

Furious lightning scratches the bloodstained sky
A never-ending portal of darkness
Twisted souls of trees loom over unwanted trespassers
The tormented sky fractures into millions of pieces
The deserted moor tortures innocent souls

Three jagged rocks swiftly rise in darkness
Blocking the travellers' path
Ghostly figures form an enchanted circle of death
Possessed souls trapped in hideous bodies
Gnarled fingers strain towards life
Hair like wire, cloaks of death
Foretelling twisted futures
Come back you imperfect speakers, tell me more!

Emily Woollcott (10)
Great Chart Primary School, Ashford

The Heath

Skeletal trees tower over travellers like a shadow
Fearless wind tears apart the land
Lightning rips open the soulless sky
Mysterious mist surrounds the deserted moorland and Macbeth
From three rugged rocks
Deformed hunchbacks are conjured
Eerie cackles throb through Macbeth's mind
Familial crows laugh at the sight
Silver mist seems to suffocate them
Smothering
Choking
Strange prophecies uttered from the strange hags
Thoughts drown in dark desires
Macbeth blinded by the midnight sky
Before these hideous witches disappear.

Chloe Worsdell (11)
Great Chart Primary School, Ashford

Macbeth

Raging thunder shakes the skies over a Scottish moor
Flashing lightning streaks across
Plunging deadly spikes into barren land
Constant rain lashes down, whipping the ground
Blasts of wind blankets of mist
Swirling around us, trapping us
Smoky grey clouds hide the moon - the moon - the moon
The glowing moon, illuminating the scene . . .

A sinister night
Mysterious stenches float around
Crooked trees peep through their branches
Withered and skeleton-like, dying by the minute
Wild wind wails at you, it says, 'Darkness hides many things . . .'

Magic creeps into every crack and crevice
Witches' magic
Conjuring up spells
Witchcraft lurks in the darkness
Creating a grim, gloomy ambiance
For all trespassers to face

Three dark shapes, silhouettes of death
Gnarled, wicked hags
Bent double like old beggars
Lean
Mean
Keen to curse and kill
Crowded round a cauldron
A bubbling, boiling cauldron
Stirring up secrets of evil . . .

Alexandra Skendros (11)
Great Chart Primary School, Ashford

Macbeth

Howling wind swirls
Darkness covers the sky like a black blanket
Lightning hunting for its prey
Thunder shouts guarding a great secret
Witches as bent as crooked branches
Their heather cloaks cover pale faces
The cauldron
Horrified
Bubbling, bubbling, bubbling
Rocks sleep silently
Trees waving for help
The stench of the living dead
Rotten grass as brown as oak wood
A mystery that is covered forever
Darkness awaits.

Mason Collen (10)
Great Chart Primary School, Ashford

Waiting . . .

Lightning illuminates like glowing candles
Reaching, reaching, reaching
For faultless victims
Blinding them

Three hunched vagabonds
Fossilised bones glaring
Grey-haired vagrants with gnarled backs
Summoning wickedness
Bubbles bubbling inside darkness

Barren land surrounding
Wind howling like ravenous wolves
Scarce, skeletal trees
Searching for trespassers like guards

Concealed secrets hiding beneath
Seeking trouble
Shadows lurking in the moors
Waiting . . .

Alexia Ciurea (10)

Great Chart Primary School, Ashford

Untitled

Darkness everywhere
Fog moving between the trees
Lightning crashing through the air
Exploding as it hits the soil
Rain drowning on the soil

Trees everywhere stripped of leaves
Branches reaching out for potion
Turning the trees hard

Witches bent over their cauldron
Potion liquid, coughing at the
Steam bubbling potion mixed by wind.

Holly White (11)
Great Chart Primary School, Ashford

Pirates

Shiver me timbers me fellow pirates
We shall set sail upon the seven seas
Upon my shoulder lays my smart parrot
I hope you haven't packed any blue cheese
In a bottle was an old treasure map
The captain said, 'Let's go ahead and sail!'
Proudly wearing my pirate patch and cap
The wind is blowing with very strong hail
With my mighty friends and very strong crew
As the buried treasure comes to our eye
The waves bang against the ship saying, 'Boo!'
The hail has now stopped from the sky
We watched the enemy walk the plank
We watched him as he very slowly sank.

Sophia Abbasi (11) & Indya Malhan (10)
Harvington Prep School, London

William Shakespeare Sonnet

Shakespeare's plays are often historical
Like Henry the VI part I, II and III
Twelfth night and some others are comical
In the Tempest, Prospero had to flee
He was born in Stratford Upon Avon
Shakespeare had three children, one girl and twins
He was sometimes called the Bard of Avon
In the dark play Hamlet, nobody wins
His plays are divided into three parts
Tragedy, comedy and history
Like Henry VI, Henry the IV have parts
Wrote narrative poems which told stories
We think he was born on St George's day
We also think he died on his birthday.

Sara Okamoto (11) & Rebeccca Wright (10)
Harvington Prep School, London

William Shakespeare

Shakespeare was born on St George's day
Which is in the month before May
He wrote many plays
Still famous today
In Holy Trinity church he lays.

Amira Hojeij (10)
Harvington Prep School, London

Shakespeare

William Shakespeare was quite a smart man
So no wonder Anne Hathaway loved him
Think of a hard poem and Shakespeare can
Some of his tragedy plays were grim
Shakespeare created Bottom the actor
His first name was Nick as I say
That was big in the comedy factor
Shakespeare was born and died on St George's day
I tell you that was a coincidence
In dear Holy Trinity church he lays
In Stratford he then had is residence
His plays will never ever change their ways
His wife lived seven years longer than him
So now you know that his life was not dim.

Hannah Noor Safi (11)
Harvington Prep School, London

William Shakespeare

S hakespeare was a wonderful man
H e was born on St George's day
A t the time he managed to write 38 plays
K ing Lear was one
E veryone knows the famous MacBeth
S usannah, Hamnet and Judith were his children
P eople loved his plays
E veryone also loves Hamlet
A nne Hathaway was his wife
R omeo and Juliet is a very well-known play
E veryone loves Shakespeare to this day.

Felicity Colley-Purohit (10)
Harvington Prep School, London

Feuding Families Start This Tale Of Woe

Never knowing the pain that entails
When crossed lovers, Juliet, Romeo
A disastrous plan, destined to fail.
This is a tragic tale of love and death.
Parted by Montague and Capulet,
They united the feud with their last breath,
Lovers filled with love from the time they met.
Who knew the couple were destined to meet
At the spectacular Capulets' ball.
If into the place he hadn't sneaked
Their love would never exist at all
But from you, my audience, I must part
So take your seats, the play's about to start!

Phoebe Critchlow
Ide Hill CE Primary School, Sevenoaks

Shakespeare

He was born in Elizabethan times
He had seven brothers and sisters
Shakespeare wrote sonnets that are just like rhymes
His birth generated lots of whispers
Shakespeare's plays were performed at the Globe Theatre
His plays lasted forever and ever
In one of his plays there is a creature
He wrote in black ink using a feather
A Midsummer Night's Dream has elves and fairies
He wrote about lots of mythical things
A Midsummer Night's Dream's creature is very hairy
Now I must come to the end of my poem
At this very second it is snowing.

Freya Baker
Ide Hill CE Primary School, Sevenoaks

Romeo, Romeo, What Have You Done?

As I watch him my eyes well with tears,
The moments we shared were joyous and fun,
I'm frightened, scared, my head filled with fears,
I kiss his lips to absorb the poison,
My heart is beating so painfully fast,
Romeo, oh why? What was your reason?
Tonight we'll be joined together at last,
Holding the dagger poised above my chest,
Pain stabs my heart as I watch my love lie,
I can't live without you, how will I rest?
I'll make the stab quick; I'm ready to die,
I close my eyes and take my final breath,
Everyone be prepared. This is my death!

Eloise Barham (11)
Ide Hill CE Primary School, Sevenoaks

Untitled

When I found my fantasy love with you
Down came a beautiful white dove called glove
When I found you I said how do you do
At that point it was only for our love
When I found you I saw your large long hat
When I saw that Rose I saw your red nose
I saw you, I did not think you were fat
You showed me your nose you began to pose
When you began to pose I thought of you lots
Then I came to your house and had some food
When you came to my house you saw pans/pots
Then I saw your friend, he was a cool dude
I did not know you were a light blue gnome
I did not know that a gnome like you flew.

Lauren Brazenell
Ide Hill CE Primary School, Sevenoaks

The Three Witches

O' fellow witches who is this Macbeth?
He will be king forever you'll see, maybe?
Who will be faced with a sword stabbing death?
Oh Mel you are such an evil lady!

Double, double toil and trouble fire burn
Witches when shall we meet in lightning?
Oh Mel when is it gonna be my turn?
Oh us witches are truly frightening
Oh why have you got a prickly beard?
It is not a beard , it is a bug, yum
Oh Macbeth what are we, you must have feared?
Oooh it is chewy like a chunk of gum!
Come Macbeth what do you need from us now
We sour the air like *whoosh! Pow! Whoosh! Pow! Pow!*

Rosie Martha Donohoe (10)
Ide Hill CE Primary School, Sevenoaks

Ziemowit's Sonnet About The Macbeth Play

Macbeth always wanted to become king,
But it meant murdering King Duncan,
He did the deed and proceeded to swing,
Cos the night before he slept very drunken,
Macbeth was made king and had a vision,
He has a sudden hallucination,
Then Macbeth's servant left with a mission,
To spread the warning through the whole nation,
Macbeth was found to be the murderer,
And the malicious Scottish came,
Killing Macbeth running on a girder,
Macbeth's story was one of utter shame,
Peace was restored to the land of Scotland,
They buried Macbeth in the seaside sand.

Ziemowit Burningham (11)

Ide Hill CE Primary School, Sevenoaks

Macbeth's Letter

To my darling wife, my dearest one,
What great and smashing news I have for you,
When walking home when the battle was done,
Three crazy witches came into view.

They hailed me great thanes and King of Scotland,
If it is true then you will be a queen,
Ruling over the moor and the sand,
My dear wife, it will be living the dream.

It can't happen if Duncan's on the throne,
Oh wife, if only he would disappear,
Then I could accept the crown as my own
And be lead through the streets to shouts and cheers.

I must depart now, my partner till death,
From your ever-loving husband, Macbeth.

Phoebe Critchlow
Ide Hill CE Primary School, Sevenoaks

Where Art Thou?

Searching the cold, misty night for my love
Standing here all this time waiting for him to come
Looking down from the balcony above
There is no other, he's the only one
My eyes darting through the darkness for him
A love kept from my father, a secret
I see a shadow in the light, so dim
It is him now, I know, I can feel it
From down below he looks up, our eyes meet
I know this is wrong but it feels so right
My heart pumps, feeling it skip a beat
Please don't let our love cause others to fight
But our two fathers despise each other
We will find a way, me and my lover.

Lucy Olivia Dent (12)
John Spendluffe Technology College, Alford

Ghosts Do Not Exist

Shall I ever believe of this nonsense?
A ghost to saunter the grounds in moonlight;
Thy brain must be stained or burning with pain;
Thy heart must not start or may have lost parts;
Thy eyes must be lame or fell down the drain;
Thou two sentinels must have lost thy art;
As the doom'd ghost does not exist my dear;
List, list, o'list, tush tush twill not appear.

Larissa Jade Vickers (13)
John Spendluffe Technology College, Alford

Sweet Revenge

My world has shattered
For what had my ears just absorbed?
This wicked, vile creature
Who has slept within our royal, ancient castle walls
Has betrayed the honour of my family!
With a liquid forged from hell in his palms
To walk up to my father whilst deep in slumber
Only to pour the most wretched and foul poison into my own father's tired ear!
With a look so grim like the devil's
Like a slithering serpent the poison must have trickled down
For now my mind is set on revenge!
For this is the start of a war.

Jamie-Lee Large (12) & Holly
John Spendluffe Technology College, Alford

Hamlet's Poem

It's a sin to kill a king,
Death and revenge it will bring,
Urgent murder is so foul,
But only brought by my mother's child,
Hands so cold come to me in figure-like form,
And tell a message o sorrow it brought,
Your uncle is the one to bring the murder so strong,
Your mother could not wait a minute,
Marriage fell hard up upon it,
Not a month passed after the service,
My fate was shown to watch my gravestone.

Brandon Goodwin (11)
John Spendluffe Technology College, Alford

To Be Or Not To Be

Shakespeare's not my favourite writer
I like other authors that are nicer
He used weird language
That causes me anguish
I might like him . . . when I am older!

Sumayyah Ali (11)
Laycock Primary School, London

The Lost Play

William Shakespeare did a lot of writing
We can see today almost everything
But, scholars are resigned
That they'll never find
'Cardenio', the only play that is missing.

Harley Jack Reynolds (11)
Laycock Primary School, London

Shakespearean Superstition

Saying one of Shakespeare's plays could make you worse,
The title is replaced by a small, little verse.
'The Scottish Play',
Is what they say.
Using the 'M' word is considered a curse.

Kathleen Estuesta

Laycock Primary School, London

Fakespeare

Some people think Shakespeare was a fraud
But their reasons are usually flawed
All the evidence
Doesn't make sense
We think that they're probably just bored!

Nylah James (10) & Hamdi
Laycock Primary School, London

I Used To Walk By The Great Green River

I used to walk by the great green river,
Looking for an old familiar face.
I sit, I think, cold and wet, I shiver,
But I know I should go back home, my place.
But my mother, father do not live there,
For they are the ones I am looking for.
They passed away, even though love we share,
I watch birds scatter away from the shore.
I sit on a log, memories come back,
They are flooding my mind, they are bad things.
I feel like screaming, I should have a slap,
The only mum and dad are in paintings.
I drown in the water, convenience,
Soon my dreary soul will be with my parents.

Zsofia Anna Olah (11)
St Edward's Royal Free Ecumenical Middle School, Windsor

School Days Pass By

The girls are gossiping and giggling.
The teachers hang about and chat away.
The boys are playing ball games and shouting.
It looks like it will be a normal day.

The first lesson and the teacher bores us
With facts that we don't want to remember.
I wish that we were going home by bus,
But school days stretch a little bit longer.

The few things that I like are break and lunch,
Because we can lie back and have a chat.
Relaxing and laughing without a hunch,
But then and again, everyone likes that.

Finally we all can head back home!
Everyone is free and we can roam.

Faye Wong (12)
St Edward's Royal Free Ecumenical Middle School, Windsor

'Tis Time

'Tis time for thee to move on 'ere the ghosts come to haunt thee.
'Tis time for thee to go home before darkness awaits.
'Tis time for thee to run or he will get thee
'Twas known for he doth terrible things to innocent souls.
'Tis time for thee to go or thee will meet a terrible fate.

Emilia Wilkowski (9)
St Edward's Royal Free Ecumenical Middle School, Windsor

The Wild Jungle

The cackle of a monkey fades away,
The piercing hiss of a snake comes by,
Soon the tiger comes to locate its prey,
Now you are face-to-face with a wild eye.

You leap out of the way and start to run,
You hear a squawk from high up in a tree,
Then see through the trees the glistening sun,
You see in a swamp a scaly body.

Kneeling on the ground, you look at the ants,
Hundreds scurrying along the mud path,
The jungle floor is covered in green plants,
But then you see the tiger's new footpath!

The wildlife in the jungle is lovely,
But you can't stay long, you soon have to flee!

Hannah Binns (11)
St Hilda's CE High School, Liverpool

The Disturbed

The blinding sun glistening over me,
Prisms of bright light dancing all around.
Gently swaying lilies for you to see,
Beyond me no water, instead there's ground.
Trees dance, rabbits hop in summer's warm breeze,
My deep water, tranquil to give you peace.
Summer warmth, a place to rest, so at ease,
My watery soul, for you a release.
Tranquillity seems like a guarantee,
Unfortunately that is not the case.
Hundreds of gawping eyes steal my beauty,
They insist on invading my own space.
I just want my place back, I need a break,
Guess who I am - of course a lovely lake.

Annabelle Lloyd (13)
St Hilda's CE High School, Liverpool

A Long Day

Walking slowly as she watches her babies,
Smiling at their little humps waggling,
Her feet sink into the sand up to her knees,
The red-hot sun sings with cheer, dazzling,
She carries blankets on her camel hump,
Lots of bags filled with treats, fruit, veg and sweets,
Her fur is shiny gold, she's tall and plump,
The people travel on her bump for seats,
Her babies carry only one blanket,
They're tired after one day of no rest,
They snuggle up to their mum once they've eaten,
Branches and leaves make their comfy nest,
They smell the scent of the warm, fiery sand
And they all dream of the peaceful brass band.

Poppy Casey (11)
St Hilda's CE High School, Liverpool

The Nature

I see the sunlight wake up on the hill,
When the green fields gleam and the songbirds sing.
The animals wake up and they stand still
The wild can start to get ready for spring.
Go and look out and watch the thriving trees,
Around the blue sky and grasses so green.
Look at the flowers blooming in the breeze,
Is this all true, or is it just a dream!
Look at the insects crawling down on land,
Unlike creatures like butterflies and ants.
They refuse to sit on my lonely hands,
But hide behind the large and loving plants.
It's time for the change of sun to moon,
I hope I will get the happiness soon.

Melita Crasta (12)
St Hilda's CE High School, Liverpool

The Tiger King

So many colours as you run past me
You are looking up to curse the blue sky
You are not as fast as a bumblebee
But you move quite swiftly as you pass by
Prowling in the jungle like a proud king
Where for art thou king, in your jungle home
The other animals praise you and sing
You hunt for meat in the jungle you roam
How is it that you can hunt from so far?
You are the predator and they are prey
You can kill people or leave a deep scar
You must do this to live another day
And so we shall have to come to an end
But readers remember he isn't your friend.

Izabel Fyne (11)
St Hilda's CE High School, Liverpool

Willow Tree

Really, Death is not something to be feared,
Dead as a doornail we shall soon all be,
Don't be scared when death's lonely face is reared,
We shall all go to a sweet willow tree,
Where all is calm and where all is peaceful,
A sanctuary where all is holy,
A world so idyllic and so blissful,
You are reunited with lost family,
You will thank Death for the long, tiring ride,
She has taken you to a fantasy,
You will be thankful that you died,
You wonder why you travelled anxiously,
Death is me, she who roams the long, tough night,
Step closer, that white light is very bright.

Carla Owens (12)
St Hilda's CE High School, Liverpool

Animals

Hanging up high is the orang-utan,
Swinging and swinging from each tree to tree,
They are endangered all because of Man,
They have wild orange hair that you can see,
Soaring above us are colourful birds,
Many different species together,
Lots of elephants travel in large herds,
Sometimes sheltering from the bad weather,
Fierce and so wild is what the tigers are,
Black and orange fur covers the creature,
To catch their prey they travel so, so far,
Amazingly beady black eyes feature,
Upon the gorgeously wondrous face,
They travel at an incredible pace.

Bethan Wilson (12)
St Hilda's CE High School, Liverpool

The Lion's Prey

The black and white prey catches its keen eye,
The clueless zebra not knowing its fate,
The brave lion creeps out cunning and sly,
Not many escape before it's too late,
The fearless lion will sneak to get near,
The lion then pounces, scaring its prey,
A zebra running from its biggest fear,
He wonders, *will this be my final day?*
The lion leaps and the zebra is caught,
Held in his clasp, no escape from his claws,
The pounding heart of the zebra, it fought,
The moment he thought *the zebra is yours,*
The silence, it pierced the air all around,
Zebra, no longer a sight or a sound.

Erin Sword-Gargan (12)
St Hilda's CE High School, Liverpool

The Monkey Poem

The playful monkey swings from tree to tree.
How happy and joyful this creature looks.
His home in the forest requires no key.
He has handmade recipes, never cooks.
When he sees his troop he quickens his pace.
He sleeps sound all night when the sun comes down.
This creature is a remarkable case.
His wild, soft fur is the colour dark brown.
The monkey has a bizarre appetite,
He eats bananas, pears, apples with ease.
He holds onto the branch of the tree tight.
So his friends in the jungle don't tease.
If one could see this mighty animal,
They would most likely be amazed to see.

Christina Gutteridge-Teso (12)
St Hilda's CE High School, Liverpool

Mother Nature

Smell the beautiful fresh air of outdoors,
Go explore the mysterious caves,
Where animals and birds nestle in moors,
Magnificent oceans crash down in waves,
Live your life and go sail the seven seas,
Go rest your head on the luscious green grass,
Taste the delicious honey made by bees,
Watch the seagulls, robins and blue tits pass,
Watch an oak tree grow from a seed,
Eat the tasty fruit from a strawbe'ry plant,
The smell of the four seasons you will need,
Live your great life without it you just can't,
Make all of your years always summery,
Go outside, make a fabulous mem'ry!

Emma Weeks (13)
St Hilda's CE High School, Liverpool

My Hobbies

I have a lot of hobbies which I love,
Like I visit the lovely countryside,
Where I see lots of birds like the white dove,
I also love horses on which I ride,
When its summertime, I love to dance,
Of a weekend I also love to act,
I also love music, it's like a trance,
I go out with my friends, we have a pact,
Anytime, everywhere I love a book,
I love flutes, as the music tends to ring,
Of an evening, I just love to cook,
These are the hobbies, which I do most days,
I'll do them always, unless it's a phase!

Georgia Norris (13)
St Hilda's CE High School, Liverpool

YoungWriters

My Heaven Will Be A Library

Sometimes books are worth gold but you can't steal,
Tales grow in our hearts like burning seeds
In a world of murder and love . . . What's real?
Curled on a sofa with a serene read.
Deluded in forests and mountains crisp,
If I'm crestfallen there'll always be love.
But there'll always be darkness in the mist,
Whilst in the twilight birds soar high above.
You'll find in a cave secrets are untold.
When leaving a close friend that you adore.
The misty mountains and forests will behold
Closing a book I never feel remorse.
When I pick up a book it feels alive,
When I'm immersed I leave the world behind.

Safia Shakil (13)
St Hilda's CE High School, Liverpool

Romeo And Juliet

Juliet was a Capulet
She loved Romeo, whom she met
Romeo was a Montague
Count Paris, Juliet saw right through

Juliet was a very pretty girl
Her resemblance was as beautiful as a pearl
Her passion was also as big as the world
Her kindred spirit made her never dull

When Juliet pretended to be dead
Her body was laid in a tomb
At the sight of her, Romeo wept
He knew she had come to her doom.

Rachel Ellen Branscombe (9)
Shrivenham CE Primary School, Swindon

Romeo And Juliet

Juliet was a Capulet
Of so long ago
Her father held a party, on this summer night
When she met the one, it suddenly turned bright
Oh Romeo, oh Romeo,
The boy of my dreams
I wish we could sail away on those streams.
Now they are dead
All stained in red.

Laura Horsfall (10)
Shrivenham CE Primary School, Swindon

Romeo And Juliet

Although they were in love, they could not talk,
They could not meet, or together walk.
From different families they were separated,
If they were together they would be hated.
Unexpectedly, Romeo fell under the spell of love,
His heart soaring, flying like a dove.
A secret wedding was arranged,
Despite Juliet suffering terrible pain.
Her cousin was murdered by her one true love,
Cousin Tybalt rose to Heaven above.
Juliet was held back, from running away,
With her family, the Capulets, she had to stay.
A plan was made, but failed to spread,
To the groom, poor Romeo ended up dead.
The plan was Juliet faked to be dead,
But Romeo thought it was real, instead.
He sacrificed his life, to be with Juliet,
And many people took that as a threat?
Juliet awoke to find him permanently asleep,
Beside his body, she started to weep.
She ended her life, to be with him,
The action she made, was the end most sin.

Charlie Jepson (10)
Shrivenham CE Primary School, Swindon

Romeo And Juliet Poem: Shakespeare

Romeo loved Rosaline, but Rosaline did not,
Romeo then found Juliet, who was super-hot,
But Juliet was from a hated family. Oh no,
But Romeo did not get sad or low,
They met in a garden, and didn't get caught,
So they both had a massive thought,
They got married, in secret of course,
But then Juliet heard something that made her voice go hoarse,
She had to marry Count Paris as arranged by her dad,
Well you could tell she was quite mad,
She took pills to make her unconscious on the day of the wedding,
They took her to a tomb without stopping,
Romeo heard the news and thought she was dead,
So he jumped out of bed,
He had been exiled for killing Juliet's cousin,
It had all happened really sudden,
Tybalt (Juliet's cousin) had killed Romeo's mate,
And then everything turned with a slate,
Romeo stabbed Tybalt's heart,
Then came the prince who was eating a tart,
He banished Romeo away,
Romeo couldn't even pray,
So when Romeo went to the tomb which held his love,
He noticed a man mourning above,
It was Count Paris, the man who would have married Juliet,
When Paris saw Romeo he started to fret,
Romeo killed him easily,
And also quickly,
He saw Juliet all cold and bland; he reached out for her hand,
And then he drank poison and left this land,
Juliet then woke with a start,
And saw dear Romeo cold at the heart,
She stabbed herself to be with him,
The next day when they had been found, the families sang a hymn,

The hated families became chums,
And didn't call each other bums
They joined other lovers who needed to be with each other.

Harvey Worden (10)
Shrivenham CE Primary School, Swindon

Easter Sonnet

Jesus prays quietly knelt on the mount
For Himself, His disciples and us all.
The disciples slept and gave no account
'Why sleep, get up and pray that you don't fall.'
A crowd appeared while He spoke out loud
Judas in front met Jesus with a kiss.
His followers saw and attacked the crowd,
A servant lost his ear. 'No more of this!'
Jesus cried. He touched and healed the man's ear.
Jesus was arrested, judged by Pilate.
The people shout, Crucify Him!' and cheer.
On the cross he dies. God takes His spirit.
Joseph placed His body in a bare tomb,
On the third day He's risen - no more gloom.

Harry Baker (11)
The King's School, Witney

An Easter Sonnet

In Gethsemane Jesus prayed to God.
He asked God if there was another way.
God looked at Jesus and began to nod.
God took a long breath then started to say,
'No, for it is written in a scripture.'
When Romans arrived he put up no fight.
Where Jesus was taken you should picture.
He was taken to Golgotha in fright!
He was hung on a cross on that cold night.
A man called Joseph put him in a cave.
And on that hot Friday all was not right.
Jesus fought death and won, for he was brave
And so we remember Easter Sunday.
We are free so rejoice in every way.

Jacob Neil (10)
The King's School, Witney

A Sensational Easter Sonnet

I know a story that you may know too.
Jesus rode a donkey to cheers of praise.
For he had an amazing job to do.
Jesus in temple with tables to raise.
Bread as his body, red wine as his blood.
Gethsemane, the air was filled with prayer.
Jesus arrested, the soldiers came in a flood.
Jesus was whipped and hurt but did not care.
He was nailed on the cross for our sin.
He said, 'It is finished,' and bowed his head.
The Romans thought they had an easy win
For they did not know that he was not dead.
From the rock tomb the stone was rolled away.
Jesus had risen and saved our today!

Joseph Biddlecombe (11)
The King's School, Witney

Romeo And Juliet

Oh, Juliet!
Her dark eyes full of love,
Her gentle skin as soft as a dove,
Her deep brown hair glistening brightly,
Her step like an angel's, ever so lightly.

Oh, Romeo!
His eyes of fiery longing
Makes me feel like I'm belonging.
His laugh, as bright and joyful as the sun
Makes me feel like he's the one.

Heather McRobbie
The Pines School, Bracknell

Beatrice And Benedick

Beatrice and Benedick,
Two ex-lovers,
One so cocky,
The other so pretty.

Never have they hated each other so very much,
Their insults and arguments so fierce,
Like a demon set on fire inside their hearts,
Hatred, silence, insult, repeat . . .

Beatrice derives the need of a husband,
Benedick thinks he can get any girl he wants,
But all they really want is each other,
And that's what they get,
A happily married life,
Without a single insult in sight.

Lottie Baxter (12)
The Redhill Academy, Nottingham

Young Writers Information

We hope you have enjoyed reading this book – and that you will continue to in the coming years.

If you're a young writer who enjoys reading and creative writing, or the parent of an enthusiastic poet or story writer, do visit our website **www.youngwriters.co.uk**. Here you will find free competitions, workshops and games, as well as recommended reads, a poetry glossary and our blog.

If you would like to order further copies of this book, or any of our other titles, then please give us a call or visit **www.youngwriters.co.uk**.

Young Writers
Remus House
Coltsfoot Drive
Peterborough
PE2 9BF
(01733) 890066 / 898110
info@youngwriters.co.uk